JOHANNES
GUTENBERG

INVENTOR OF THE PRINTING PRESS

SPECIAL LIVES IN HISTORY THAT BECOME

Signature LIVES

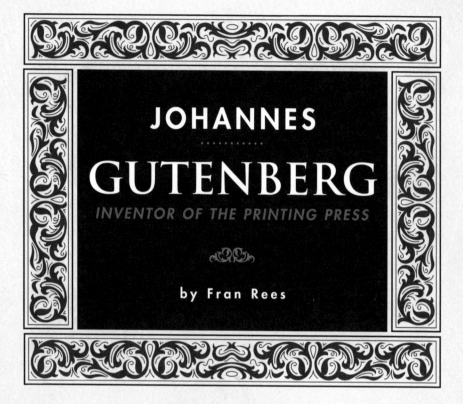

JOHANNES
GUTENBERG

INVENTOR OF THE PRINTING PRESS

by Fran Rees

Content Adviser: Frank Romano, Professor Emeritus,
Rochester Institute of Technology,
Rochester, New York

Reading Adviser: Rosemary G. Palmer, Ph.D.,
Department of Literacy, College of Education,
Boise State University

COMPASS POINT BOOKS ✦ MINNEAPOLIS, MINNESOTA

Compass Point Books
3109 West 50th Street, #115
Minneapolis, MN 55410

Visit Compass Point Books on the Internet at *www.compasspointbooks.com*
or e-mail your request to *custserv@compasspointbooks.com*

Editor: Sue Vander Hook
Lead Designer: Jaime Martens
Page Production: Bobbie Nuytten
Photo Researchers: Jo Miller and Svetlana Zhurkin
Cartographer: XNR Productions, Inc.
Educational Consultant: Diane Smolinski

Managing Editor: Catherine Neitge
Creative Director: Keith Griffin
Editorial Director: Carol Jones

Library of Congress Cataloging-in-Publication Data
Rees, Fran
  Johannes Gutenberg / by Fran Rees
    p. cm—(Signature lives)
  Includes bibliographical references and index.
ISBN 0-7565-0989-0 (hardcover)
  1. Gutenberg, Johann, 1397?–1468—Juvenile literature. 2. Printers—
Germany—Biography—Juvenile literature. I. Title. II. Series.
  Z126.Z7R44 2006
  070.5'092—dc22   2005004613

Signature Lives

RENAISSANCE ERA

The Renaissance was a cultural movement that started in Italy in the early 1300s. The word *renaissance* comes from a Latin word meaning "rebirth," and during this time, Europe experienced a rebirth of interest and achievement in the arts, science, and global exploration. People reacted against the religion-centered culture of the Middle Ages to find greater value in the human world. By the time the Renaissance came to a close, around 1600, people had come to look at their world in a brand new way.

Table of Contents

1 FACING DEFEAT

❧✿❧

Johannes Gutenberg paced the floor of his workshop. Several printing presses stood against the walls, and large sheets of print hung from the ceiling to dry. A chilling wind blew off the Rhine River and seeped through the windows. The sky was gray. It was November 6, 1455, in Mainz, Germany.

Nervously, Gutenberg picked up one of the sheets and held it near the window. He looked with concern at the beautiful lines of thick, black type so neatly printed in columns. He walked to a table where stacks of finished sheets lay dry and folded. There was a chance he could lose it all today. His financial partner, Johann Fust, was in court at that very moment, asking a judge to give him everything in Gutenberg's workshop.

Johannes Gutenberg at his printing press

Gutenberg was proud of his work, his marvelous printing press, and the pages of the Bible he had finished printing. He had poured more than 20 years of his life and his entire fortune into his printing press. He had also borrowed a lot of money from Fust and others to make his dream possible. The press was just what he wanted it to be—a remarkable invention that would serve mankind and God. If only he knew for certain he would be able to print more copies of the Bible. If only he could present his work to the world, sell books, and recover the money he had already spent. If only ...

Gutenberg continued to pace around the workshop. Earlier that day, he had sent his trusted assistants, Heinrich Keffer and Bechtolf von Hanau, to the Convent of the Barefoot Friars in Mainz. The court case against him was being heard there. The charge was failure to repay his debt to Fust. The outcome of the trial would change his life, but he had decided not to attend.

Any moment now, the judge would announce the verdict Gutenberg was anxiously awaiting. Heinrich and Bechtolf surely would return soon with the news. They would tell him whether or not Johann Fust had won the case against him. Would Gutenberg lose his invention and all his work? At this point, he could only hope the judge would rule in his favor.

A plaintiff and a defendant kneel before the judge in a 15th-century court

Suddenly the door opened, and a gust of wind blew into the workshop. Gutenberg shivered when he felt the cold and shuddered deep in his heart when he saw the long, sad faces of his assistants. What they told him was not good. The judge had ruled in favor of Fust, and Gutenberg had lost. He had lost it all.

He struggled with the news. How could everything be taken from him, even his presses and his equipment? What about the thousands of sheets of printed pages that were ready to be bound into 175

Bibles? Heinrich and Bechtolf informed him that everything now belonged to Fust and his partner, Peter Schöffer.

Gutenberg's worst fear had now come true. He had known the court might rule in Fust's favor. His fear had even kept him at his workshop during the trial. He could not bear to face the judge, so he had sent his two most loyal craftsmen instead. Nevertheless, it was all over. He was defeated by his own partner.

Gutenberg knew he had no recourse, nowhere else to turn for help. He had borrowed money from Fust again and again. Time after time, he had used up the money to buy expensive metals and pay the workmen to set the type and work the presses. It had taken a great deal of money to buy the parchment and paper, discover the right ingredients for the ink, and build the presses. He had not been able to repay Fust, not even a cent of it.

But why couldn't Fust wait just a little longer? Why did he want all the money back right now, just when so many copies of the Bible were printed and ready to be bound into books? Why couldn't Fust wait until the work was completely finished—when they could begin to make some money from the sale of the Bibles?

But Fust and Schöffer didn't care about Gutenberg. They had won their case, and now they

Johannes Gutenberg examines a page printed on his printing press.

could go on to finish the project themselves. They would bind and sell the Bibles, print other books, and profit from Gutenberg's work and invention. Fust and Schöffer took every piece of equipment and every printed page from Gutenberg's workshop and set up their own business. In the following years, they printed many books and put their special mark, or logo, on them that identified them as the printer. Their business soon became a great success.

Gutenberg's name never appeared on any copies of the Bible he had printed, nor did he ever make any money from his lifelong project. Some of the men Gutenberg had trained in his printing process went to other cities and built their own printing presses. Printing workshops sprang up all over Europe. But it would be many years before Gutenberg received credit for his marvelous invention.

On that sad day, however, when Gutenberg received word of his defeat, he didn't know what the far-reaching power of his invention would be. He could not have known that his ideas would spread quickly throughout Europe and become the standard process for printing for the next 400 years.

Printing gave rise to a new era and shaped the course of civilization. Over the next 45 years, more than 10 million books were printed. Never before had so much knowledge been so available. As books became affordable, more and more people learned to read and

The Renaissance was an era of discovery and learning. Four men stand out for their outstanding contributions to this era. Christopher Columbus journeyed to the "ends of the earth" and proved that the world was round. Nicolas Copernicus proved Earth revolved around the sun, not the other way around. Martin Luther brought about a religious revolution. Johannes Gutenberg provided a method of printing that made new ideas and discoveries available to everyone.

owned books.

Gutenberg's dream was taken from him before it came true. In one sense, he went down in defeat, never to fully recover from his loss. But history has been kind to him and has credited him with one of the greatest inventions of all time.

Fust and Schöffer may have profited from the printing press and the Bible, but history only remembers them for taking credit for what was rightfully Gutenberg's. People at that time knew who had really invented the printing press—Gutenberg. In the 16th century, even one of Schöffer's descendants gave Gutenberg credit as the inventor. Historians throughout the years have investigated documents and debated who actually invented the printing press. Most agree it was Gutenberg.

The words *printing press* and *Gutenberg* are forever linked, and Johannes Gutenberg made his imprint on history after all. ℘

Johannes Gutenberg (1398?-1468)

2 GROWING UP IN MAINZ

ೋ⌒ೋ

Johannes Gutenberg was about 55 years old when he lost his printing press and his printed pages of the Bible. By that time, he had already lived a full and interesting life in Germany. His family was well known in the town of Mainz, where Johannes was born in about 1398. No one knows for sure the exact date of his birth.

Johannes grew up in a wealthy home. His father, Friele Gensfleisch, was a member of the aristocracy, the wealthy, powerful people who owned land and governed the town. Johannes' mother, Else Wirich Gutenberg, was also a highly respected landowner. Johannes lived with his parents, an older brother, and a sister in a home called the Gutenberg House, once owned by his mother's ancestors.

Dinner was an extravagant affair for wealthy European families.   **17** ೋೋ

Gutenberg was not Johannes' last name. In Europe, there were no family names that could be handed down from father to son and grandson. If people were known by anything other than their first names, it was usually the name of their house or the property the family owned.

At that time, a house or a piece of property was given a name, which stayed the same for several hundred years. Johannes sometimes went by Gensfleisch, the name of his father's childhood home. But there were several others named Johannes in Mainz who were also of the house of Gensfleisch. So he usually used Gutenberg, the name of the house he lived in.

Johannes' house was large, with an inner courtyard where trees and flowers could grow. It was not just Johannes' family of five who lived there. Aunts, uncles, and cousins made the Gutenberg House their home as well.

Life in the early 1400s was very hard and different from our world today. Gutenberg lived his entire life in two German cities, Mainz and Strasbourg, located about 100 miles (160 kilometers) apart. There were few modern conveniences, and methods of travel and communication were not advanced. People didn't read newspapers and magazines to find out what was happening, because none existed. There was no way to print something on paper other than writing by hand, so news spread by word of mouth. Travelers and storytellers gathered with townspeople at inns and taverns to describe what

Merchants of Mainz, Germany, selling their goods on the streets

was going on in the rest of the world.

Even the wealthiest of homes had few conveniences. There was no electricity, refrigeration, or indoor plumbing. A large chamber pot that resembled a ceramic bowl was used for a toilet. When it needed to be emptied, the contents were poured out an upper floor window onto the street. People walking along the streets of Mainz had to be watchful and very careful. Also, since there was no running water in houses, people took baths in public or private bathhouses located throughout the city.

Wealthy families were fortunate to have candlelight in their houses. Because candles were expensive, poorer citizens could not afford them and had to get by with just the light from the fireplace. Few homes had glass windows. Most were covered with heavy wooden shutters that helped keep out the cold but also made the houses quite dark inside. Fireplaces were the only source of heat. In the tightly closed homes, especially in the winter, the fires left the houses

Mainz, Germany, was part of the Holy Roman Empire and governed by an archbishop of the Roman Catholic Church. The archbishop was allowed to make gold coins to be used as money. This attracted many highly skilled goldsmiths and metal craftsmen to the city to work. Mainz became famous for its jewelry, gold, silverwork, and metal polishing. The city's Latin name was Aurea Moguntia, which means Golden Mainz.

dirty with soot and smelling of smoke.

Mainz was a bustling commercial town and one of the richest, most important cities along the Rhine River. It was not unusual for Johannes to walk along the busy riverfront and see many boats and ships full of cargo. Workers would be busy unloading crates onto the docks. Every day, large cranes swung bales of cloth onto the shore, where merchants came to pick up their goods.

The riverbank at Mainz, Germany, was a busy place, where ships delivered goods daily.

The city was well known for its fine metalwork. People came from all over to buy coins, jewelry, and other items made of fine metals like gold and silver. The sound of goldsmiths clanging metal upon metal rang out from the local shops.

Above the city walls, tall spires rose sharply from the tops of roofs and pointed to the sky. Johannes and his friends played in the streets beneath the wood-tiled roofs of the houses that dotted the hillsides. In the middle of it all loomed the tall tower of St. Martin's Cathedral, whose church

Many people in Mainz, Germany, worked as goldsmiths, making fine gold and silver jewelry.

bells rang out many times during the day.

Getting around in Mainz was not easy. The streets were winding, rough, and often filled with mud. Horse-drawn carts wound their way through the narrow lanes, while people rushed around on foot. On his way to school, Johannes would have walked down twisting streets that curved around and between tall, narrow buildings. On the bottom floor of these buildings were shops and businesses. People lived above them in the upper floors that jutted out over the street to create more living space. Pigs, chickens, and other animals ate garbage that was tossed into ditches. When Johannes walked down the street, he had to watch where he stepped to avoid the rubbish along the way.

For many centuries, only the privileged few had received an education. Boys and young men who went to school usually attended a Roman Catholic monastery, where they were trained to become priests or monks. If girls received an education, it was usually in a convent, where they lived to fulfill their religious vows. But by the time Johannes was born, schools were being established all over Europe. Many children were starting their education at an early age. Schools taught grammar, reading, simple math, and clear speaking, called discourse.

Even though there were many schools, there were very few books. Often only the teacher had a copy of the schoolbooks. Children were taught by questions and answers. The teacher asked a question, and the students chanted the answer together.

When Johannes was a young man, most European books were written by hand with quill and ink and then bound in workshops. At that time, the desire for information, education, and knowledge about the world was increasing rapidly, so copying books became a profitable business. But it was hard for the scribes who copied each book to keep up with the demand. Most scribes were priests or monks who worked many hours each day in a scriptorium carefully copying each word and each page of a book by hand. It was a slow process and could take a single scribe up to five months to complete one book.

Scribes wrote the words on loose sheets of parchment, a material made from the dried and treated skins of calves, goats, or sheep. The skins had to be soaked, stretched, and scraped until they were thin and smooth enough to write on. After the words were written on parchment, the pages were decorated with designs, borders, and miniature scenes. A giant, colorful letter called a versal sometimes marked the beginning of a chapter. Brightly colored, hand-painted pictures and thin bits of real gold or silver made the pages of a book shiny. That is how they came to be called illuminated manu-

A scribe's job of copying books by hand was a long, slow process.

scripts. When the pages were completed, the book-seller put them in the correct order, sewed them together by hand where they folded in the center, and bound them in a cover.

Johannes was growing up at a time when things were changing rapidly in Europe. People wanted to learn more about religion, law, science, philosophy, geography, and the happenings of their day. The demand for books was growing all over Europe. More and more scribes were hired to copy books, and they were asked to work faster and faster.

Sometimes the writing was hard to read, and the hurried scribes made mistakes. Books could not be handmade quickly enough.

Wealthy people, churches, and libraries owned most of the books. Johannes probably went with his father to the local monastery or university library to read books. Books were so valuable and costly that they were chained to tables or high shelves so they could not be removed from the room.

All books were chained to tables at the University of Leyden in Germany.

Most of the people who made books belonged to a guild, a group of merchants or craftsmen with a similar skill and occupation. There were guilds for carpenters, blacksmiths, shoemakers, goldsmiths,

bakers, and others. Guild members were part of the working class, not educated or wealthy like the landowners. They made things with their hands, managed the shops that sold their goods, and set the standards for their trade. They were important to the local economy.

Some of the guilds decided to come together and form one large guild, much like a present-day labor union. That way, they could have more influence and power in the city. Some guild members even gained positions in local government and served on the city council.

The men in Johannes' family were not guild members. They belonged to a group of high-ranking city leaders known as patricians. Usually, patricians didn't have to work, since they had inherited a great deal of money and property. Many of them held positions on the city council. They far outnumbered the guild members who held government positions.

Patricians were in charge of collecting taxes and managing the mint, where coins were made. Gutenberg's father was a member of Mainz's city council and also in charge of the mint. Soon, Johannes would realize that people looked down on him and his family because of his father's political position. ✑

Chapter
3   EXILED

ec×ン

In 1411, when Johannes Gutenberg was about 13 years old, he learned what it was like to be hated. In the winter of 1410–1411, Johannes and his family were forced to flee Mainz and live in the country for their own safety. The family packed up everything that would fit in their horse-drawn carriages and quickly left the only home and city Johannes had ever known. The people forcing them to leave were the working class, the guild members.

As one large organization, the guilds in Mainz had become more and more powerful over the years. The wealthy patricians and the poorer guild members didn't always get along. Guild members felt they didn't have enough say in city government, and the number of patricians on the city council still

The carpenter's guild was one of many groups of craftsmen in Germany.

outnumbered the guild. The guild protested against how much power the wealthy patrician families had, and they wanted lower taxes.

That winter was a long, bitter one in Mainz. Many working people were not earning enough money to keep their families fed and warm. When the council voted to raise taxes, guild members became angrier than ever. They stormed into the town hall, physically threw out the patricians, and took over the city's government. Johannes' father lost his position on the council and his job at the mint. Working people made it very clear that wealthy patrician families were not welcome in Mainz.

What an impression this must have made on young Johannes! Just being a member of an important, wealthy family did not always mean he would have security. He had to think about what he might do with his life. Perhaps he decided then and there to learn a trade.

For three years, Johannes lived away from the noise, dirt, and bad smells of Mainz. No one knows what life was like for him during those years in the country. But after three years, when Johannes was about 16, his family moved back to the city. The patricians and guilds had come to peaceful terms with one another, so it was safe to live in Mainz once again.

A patrician couple is dressed for an important occasion.

Johannes' father returned to work at the mint but did not become a member of the town council again. Although Johannes did not have to work for money, he decided to learn a craft, in case he did not always have his family's wealth to fall back on. He joined his father in the mint and learned to make gold coins. As a goldsmith, Johannes had to learn metallurgy, the science of metals. He was taught how gold was refined, melted, molded, and engraved. When the gold was hot, Johannes learned how to pour it into a form shaped like a coin. When it cooled down just enough, he stamped a special

A mint in Germany where gold and silver coins were molded and stamped

mark onto the metal and engraved tiny words and emblems on it with special tools.

Learning this mixture of science and art prepared Johannes for what he would do many years later—design and build a printing press. He would be able to form metal molds for each letter of the alphabet, pour in molten metal, and shape each one to perfection with metal tools. These metal bars of type, as they were called, became the basis for printing an entire page and then an entire book.

Gutenberg worked alongside his father at the mint for many years. Then in 1419, his father died. Gutenberg, now about 21, continued to work at the mint and improve his skills with metals for the next nine years.

There were many other things for Johannes to learn at this time when knowledge and information were so available. This period of history came to be called the Renaissance, a word that means rebirth. It was a time when people had a thirst for knowledge, art, and exploration like the world had not seen in hundreds of years. Renaissance thinkers paid attention to subjects such as history, poetry, public speaking, and other languages. New ideas that were being discussed during the Renaissance caused people to question what they had believed about religion. For many years, people had centered their thoughts on life after death; now people concentrated on making their earthly life better.

Gutenberg studied many subjects, probably at one of the nearby German universities. He knew the Latin language and later used that knowledge to print the Bible in accurate Latin. He also discovered new paper shops that had opened in town. Paper mills in Mainz were producing lots of paper, and for the first time, people could buy it for their personal use. This might have been the time Gutenberg began to form his ideas for printing on paper.

Robed students attend class at a 15th-century university.

In 1428, there were more troubles in the city of Mainz. The guilds were again demanding lower taxes. They also wanted to stop some of the wealthy families from owning property in the city. The patricians and guilds argued; some of the patricians even argued among themselves. When the disagreements got heated, certain patrician families refused to stay in Mainz and moved to their country estates. Others decided to stay in the city and cooperate with the powerful guilds.

Gutenberg was one of those who refused to stay. Once more, he left his hometown because of political troubles. This time, he decided to settle in Strasbourg, Germany, where he would set up a business in a more stable and friendly environment. ❧

4 MAN OF MYSTERY

⌒⌒⌒

The city of Strasbourg was more modern than Mainz. It was a charming city with stone-paved streets and the River Ill running through it. The massive Strasbourg Cathedral stood majestically in the middle of town, with towers so tall they almost vanished into the mist that hung heavily in the sky. The cathedral was a masterpiece of Western art. The finest handwritten books of the day filled its library.

In Strasbourg, Gutenberg was sort of a man of mystery. For more than 20 years, he lived and worked there, but no one knew much about him or what he was doing. Sometime while he was there, he began experimenting with printing and making books. He must have tested and developed his method for printing words onto paper.

Completed in 1439, the Strasbourg Cathedral in Strasbourg, Germany (now France), became the world's tallest building.

But those years leave many questions. When did he invent the amazing but simple handheld mold for each letter of the alphabet? How did he mold and chisel each bar of type? When did he discover how to place the type in a chase, to make an entire page of sentences? How did he learn to mix the right ingredients together to make ink that would stick to

Gutenberg's printing press, chase, handheld molds, and copies of his printed books

paper and yet not smudge? How long did it take to build the printing press and print his first book? How many people worked with him? How many people knew his secret?

Gutenberg lived just outside the city walls in the old monastery of St. Arbogast, a quiet place suitable for working on his invention. Here he had privacy and could use a forge, a very hot open furnace used to melt gold and other metals. Forges were forbidden within the city walls because they were a fire hazard.

Gutenberg spent some of his time in the city making business contacts and building friendships. People knew him as a goldsmith and a member of the upper class. He was also known as a successful businessman who dealt in precious metals and wine. City records show that in 1439 he paid taxes on about 528 gallons (2,006.4 liters) of wine, which he probably sold or traded in one of his businesses.

Not all of his business contacts were good, however. Gutenberg ended up in court several times over bad business deals. One time, he took a man to court to force him to pay a debt. In another case, a woman took Gutenberg to court, claiming he did not keep his promise to marry her. But Gutenberg won the case and did not have to pay the woman any money. There is no record that Gutenberg ever did get married. Others sued him for not repaying money he had borrowed for his business projects.

The man of mystery was very good at keeping his work a secret. He and his partners, who had invested some of their money in his work, had very good reasons to keep quiet. In those days, there was no way to obtain complete rights to an invention. Because Gutenberg's printing press could easily be copied if someone saw how it worked, it was extremely important to guard the secret. When Gutenberg went to court once for not paying his debts, even his witnesses were secretive about what he was doing. They revealed as little information as possible. They referred to the project as "it," "art and adventure," or "art and invention." Sometimes it was just the "enterprise."

In 1433, five years after he moved to Strasbourg, Gutenberg returned to Mainz for his mother's funeral, but he did not stay. He went back to Strasbourg, expecting that he would soon get the money his mother and father had left him as his inheritance. But he learned it was going to be hard to get his money out of Mainz. The

Gutenberg was not the only person to guard the secrets of his work. In the 15th century, trade secrets were guarded closely. Bakers did not reveal their recipes, and jewelers kept their techniques to themselves. A patent, the right to be the only one allowed to use an invention or process, did not exist in Gutenberg's day. Therefore, the only way to keep others from stealing an invention was to keep it secret.

money was held by the city, and since Gutenberg did not live there, the city avoided paying him. City leaders wanted him to spend his money there, not in Strasbourg.

Gutenberg was angry with officials in Mainz. He needed money to pursue his work. When he left Mainz, Gutenberg asked Niklaus von Worrstadt, one of the city officials, to handle the money the city owed him. One day, Gutenberg learned that Worrstadt was in Strasbourg. He got together some

Cities, businesses, and wealthy families hired bookkeepers to handle their money.

Caſſier ambt Jch verrichten ſoll/
Mit ein vnd auſzgeben gar wol.
Die Caſſa Jch offt vberſchlag/
Vnd den Reſt fleiſſig bey mir trag.

of his powerful friends, and they demanded that Worrstadt pay him the money. Worrstadt must have refused, because he was thrown into debtor's prison, where people who couldn't pay their debts were locked up. When Worrstadt arranged for the city of Mainz to pay Gutenberg, he was released from prison and given his freedom.

After this incident, Gutenberg became known as a man "who counted: hard-nosed, decisive, but fair-minded. A man to watch." Gutenberg received only part of his money from the city of Mainz, but he had enough to pay his workers and fund the work he was doing in his workshop for a while. Eventually, he would need more money to finance his invention. He was a respectable citizen in his mid-30s with good contacts in the community, and some people knew he was engaged in some important work.

He often trained other people to help him cut and polish precious metals and stones. One of his pupils was a prominent citizen named Andreas Dritzehn. By 1438, Dritzehn had learned the craft well enough to become Gutenberg's partner. Two other men, Hans Riffe and Andreas Heilmann, also joined him as partners. They invested money in Gutenberg's business and joined him in a very different moneymaking venture—the sale of mirrors.

Mirrors were a new item in Europe. The men decided to make a special kind of mirror that would be sold as an item with miraculous powers. They planned to sell thousands of mirrors at a holy event taking place in Aachen, Germany.

The Aachen event was a special occasion that took place once every seven years. Pilgrims traveled from all over to attend the event that was called a fair. The next pilgrimage was scheduled in 1439 near the French and German border, about 300 miles (480 km) from Strasbourg. Thousands of people would make the journey to Aachen. They would come to catch a glimpse of precious relics believed to be the cloths that baby Jesus was wrapped in at birth. They

A German country fair

also hoped to see the clothing of Mary, the mother of Jesus. Even the clothes that Jesus wore at his crucifixion were supposed to be there.

To protect the relics, fair officials would only let people look at them from a distance, at a place between two tall buildings. If the pilgrims had mirrors, they might be able to catch a reflection of the relics. It was believed that by catching a mirror image of something holy, part of its holiness stayed with you forever.

The story goes that Gutenberg and his partners worked for months making mirrors for the Aachen event. They planned to make a lot of money on this enterprise. The mirrors were not costly to make, and they could charge quite a bit for each one.

However, the businessmen's hard work never paid off. After making thousands of mirrors, they learned that the Aachen pilgrimage had been postponed until the following year. A fatal disease called the bubonic plague, or the Black Death, was spreading rapidly throughout the country. People had to stay away from anyone who had this contagious disease. This was devastating news for Gutenberg and his partners. They had already spent a lot of money making the mirrors, and now there was no one to buy them, at least not for at least another year.

The men were not happy with the turn of events. They wanted to make up for the money they had

The plague killed thousands of people throughout Europe over several centuries.

lost. Gutenberg was in a difficult position. Should he let his partners work with him on his secret invention? Should he return to Mainz where he could receive more of his inheritance? He was getting close to figuring out how his printing press would work. What should he do?

He decided to let his partners in on his secret. After all, he had already trained them in the art of cutting and polishing metals and stones. Men with these skills could design the letters of the alphabet and mold them into metal bars of type. Maybe his partners would also invest money in his venture. He needed more money anyway to iron out a few problems with the process. Gutenberg made the men promise to keep everything a secret. He even drew up an agreement for them to sign. It stated that "if

Johannes Gutenberg shows his associates one of his printed pages.

any partner died before the contract ended in 1443, no new partners could join."

Later that same year, 1438, Dritzehn died of the plague. His brothers asked Gutenberg to take them on as partners in place of their brother. But Gutenberg wanted to protect his secret, and he turned them down. He also tried frantically to retrieve a piece of equipment Dritzehn had taken to his home before he died. Gutenberg was probably worried that someone might discover what he was doing if they figured out how to use the equipment. He ordered Dritzehn's family to take it apart. He also ordered them to melt down another item, perhaps a metal bar of type. Gutenberg seemed to be in a panic about anyone finding out about it.

The brothers weren't happy that they couldn't be Gutenberg's partners, and they took him to court. Again, witnesses for Gutenberg were secretive about the work he was doing. Their testimonies were vague, and they used general terms for Gutenberg's equipment. After about a year, the court ruled in Gutenberg's favor, and he quietly went back to his workshop. ❧

5 COMPLETING THE PROCESS

❧⟨✕⟩☙

Gutenberg worked hard on his invention while he was in Strasbourg. He was on the brink of finishing a new, faster way of copying books. Although no one had ever developed a printing process like his, others had experimented with printing.

Hundreds of years earlier, in the eighth century, people in China, Japan, and Korea were printing, using blocks of wood or stone on which symbols were carved. Later, they carved single characters of the Chinese alphabet on wooden blocks so they could use them again and again to form words and sentences. In 770, Japanese Empress Shotoku commissioned craftsmen to print 1 million copies of prayers. The prayers were printed on long rolls of paper called scrolls. Producing the prayer scrolls

The Chinese used movable type carved from wooden blocks as early as 1043.

took 157 men six years to complete.

In China during the 11th century, a man named Pi Sheng had an idea for making individual characters that could be moved around to make words and sentences. In this process called movable type, he first made characters out of clay and baked them. Then he chose the characters he needed, put them in a frame, spread ink on them, and pressed the inked shapes against a cloth or paper. The characters transferred to the paper and became a printed page. Later, the Chinese traced these same characters onto wooden blocks that could be carved into character shapes. The wooden blocks were used later as a form for letters that were molded out of hot metal.

There was one big problem, however. The Chinese alphabet was nothing like European letters. Europeans used a 26-letter alphabet, while the Chinese language used tens of thousands of characters. Chinese was compli-

The invention of paper was an important discovery that made printing less expensive. Paper was invented in China in 105 A.D., by a man named Ts'ai Lun. To make paper, Ts'ai Lun boiled mulberry bark, hemp, rags, and old fishnets in a pot. He then mashed the soft materials, laid the substance out in a thin layer across a mesh screen, and placed the material in the sun to dry. The stiff, dry sheet could absorb ink and be folded without breaking. In the 8th century, Arab soldiers learned how to make paper from their Chinese prisoners. In the 11th century, the first European paper mill was built in Spain.

cated, and it took too much work and time to make enough characters for printing.

Following the method developed by the Chinese, Koreans became the first to produce a system of movable metal type in 1234. Because the Korean language used a simpler version of the Chinese characters, it was easier to make the shapes. However, the Korean language still had 40,000 characters, and printing in that language was not any faster than writing by hand. Because the Chinese and Korean

A Chinese printer rubs paper pressed on top of inked blocks to make a printed page.

languages contained so many characters, printing was very difficult and not widely used.

Beginning in about 1400, people in Italy and Holland were also experimenting with movable type. Some of them claimed to be the first to invent printing in Europe. A man in Holland was quite involved with a printing process, but since his name was never known, he was not given credit for the invention of printing.

Gutenberg's experiments began in about 1435. His method eventually became the standard for printing in Europe. It was not just one invention; it was several. The printing process required numerous pieces of equipment. Gutenberg created a small handheld mold for each letter of the alphabet, called a type. He also developed a chase to hold the metal bars of type. This metal tray held the bars of type firmly in place so they would not move. Then he made a press that would put pressure evenly but firmly on a piece of paper placed over the chase.

There were several other techniques that also had to be worked out. He had to find just the right formula for ink so it would spread evenly over metal bars of type and not be too thick or too thin. The ink had to stick to the paper and dry quickly without smearing. There was also a process that made the paper suitable for printing. Paper had to be smooth, but not so slick that ink wouldn't adhere to it.

Gutenberg's equipment and processes all worked together to create pages of text that could be printed over and over. The first step was to design a style of letter. At that time, thick black Gothic letters with fancy edges were common. Gutenberg came up with a clever way to make the metal bars of type in the shape of letters.

First, a letter was chiseled and shaped to make it stand up in relief on a steel bar called a punch. The punch was used to pound a sunken impression of the letter into a brass square called a matrix. The matrix fit into the bottom of an adjustable mold, and molten lead was poured in. When the lead cooled, the hinged mold was opened, and the finished letter, or type, was removed. The edges of the letter stood above the base of the metal bar. For each letter of the alphabet, Gutenberg made many bars. Each page of text would use the same letter many times.

Gutenberg made a molded bar of type for each letter, punctuation mark, and blank space.

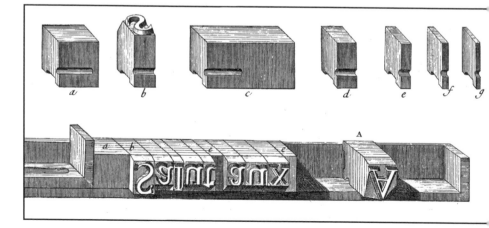

The brilliance of Gutenberg's invention was in the adjustable mold he created. This handheld mold could be changed to different widths. Because not all letters are the same width, the bars had to vary. If the letter *M* was being made, the mold had to be made wider. If the letter *I* was being made, the mold would be adjusted to make a narrower bar.

Gutenberg made bars with numbers, capital letters, lowercase letters, and large decorative letters called versals. Usually versals were used to mark the beginning of a chapter and make the page look more attractive. He also made many bars of type that were not letters. He made type for punctuation marks and even blank bars, called spacers, for the spaces between words in the text.

Making a letter took great care and accuracy. All the letters had to stand above the metal base at exactly the same height. All this was possible by using the hand mold, a real breakthrough for Gutenberg's invention.

A person called a compositor placed each bar of type into a chase to make words and sentences in mirror image.

A printer inspects a chase filled with bars of type.

After Gutenberg chose the letters he needed to make sentences and paragraphs, he placed them into a chase about the size of the page he would print. This form held the letters tightly together to keep them from shifting. The slightest movement would cause the letters to blur or smear. The letters were placed in the chase in a mirror image—backward and read from right to left. That way, when the letters were transferred with ink onto the printed page, they would be turned the correct way and could be read from left to right.

Now the chase was placed into an iron bed, a flat, shallow, boxlike metal frame. The sides were pushed together to hold the chase firmly in place. The metal bars of type had to stick up above the edges of the frame. Otherwise, when the press came down on the letters, the edges of the frame would also make an imprint.

Next, it was time to use the press, which was not a new invention. Different varieties of presses already existed in Europe. Winemakers had been using large wooden presses for centuries to crush grapes and extract the juices. But a press for printing could not be as simple as a wine press. It had to press down on the paper with a certain even pressure, and it could not move from side to side once it touched the paper.

Gutenberg got some ideas for his printing press from the way wine presses were made.

Gutenberg and his partners hired a man named Conrad Saspach to build a press that would work for

printing. The large printing press had wooden screws that, when turned, forced a large plate down over the paper. The force of the press was equal over every part of the page so every letter and punctuation would print evenly.

Gutenberg had to solve another important issue: What type of ink should he use? The ink had to be thick and dark enough to make a clear imprint. It had to stick to the metal type without running but stay wet long enough to transfer to the paper. It had to be thin enough so it would make a letter and not a blob. He also had to make ink that would not fade over time. Gutenberg experimented with various combinations of ingredients and various processes before he found just the right formula. The ink that worked best was made from linseed oil and a fine soot called lampblack.

Then Gutenberg had to decide what paper he would use. He did not intend to use parchment for the printing of most of his books. It was too expensive, and the process of preparing animal skins took too much time. Gutenberg tested different types of paper by trial and error. Paper used by scribes worked well with quill and ink, but the ink used in Gutenberg's printing process did not stick to that type of paper. The right paper had to be dampened slightly so the ink would sink in just enough. If the paper was too dry, the ink wouldn't hold. If the

The paper mill at Nuremberg, Germany, produced some of the finest paper available in Europe in the 1400s.

paper was too wet, the ink would dissolve or appear light and fuzzy.

Gutenberg was very careful to make the pages of printed text look good. This meant he had to place the letters, spacers, and borders a certain way. He also was careful to make the distance between letters and words and the borders around the page even and attractive. He had to determine how many lines on a page would be easy to read and how close the letters should be to each other. Because of his desire for precision, he was able to print pages that had a lot of words but were still easy to read.

The workshop was very large. It had to have room to store hundreds of metal bars of type and several printing presses. There had to be plenty of space where large sheets of paper could be hung up to dry. Workers were needed to help with each stage of the printing process, from setting the type to running the presses.

By the time Gutenberg's printing presses began running, his workshop was like a small manufacturing plant. Not only was he an inventor, he was also a smart businessman, a skilled manager, and a productive manufacturer. ℘

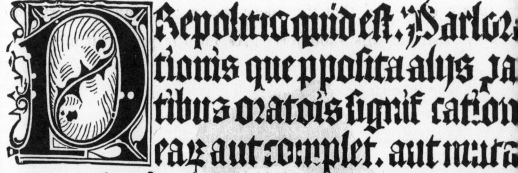

Repositio quid est.¶Parlo=
tionis que pposita alijs pa=
tibuz oratois signif catioe
eaz aut coplet. aut mutat
aut minuit.Prepositioi quot accidit
Unuz. Quid? Casus tm. Quot casus
Duo. Qui? Actus 7 abltus. Da ppo=
sitiones acti casus: ut ad. apud. ante
aduersum. cis. etra. circu. circa. cotra
erga. extra. inter. intra. infra. iuxta. o
pone. per. pe. pter. scdm. post. trans
vltra. preter. supra. circiter. vsqz. secus
penes. Quo dicimus eni? Ad patre
apud villa. ante edes. aduersum inn

6 SUCCESS AT LAST

⊶✦⊷

In 1444, Strasbourg faced the threat of war, and it was becoming dangerous to live in the city. About that time, Gutenberg fulfilled a five-year contract with his partners and had no obligations that would force him to stay there. So he decided to leave Strasbourg. For the next four years, no one knows where Gutenberg was or what he was doing. What he did with his invention during those four years is a mystery.

By 1448, Gutenberg was back in Mainz trying to collect the rest of the money from his inheritance. He wanted to set up another printing workshop. No one was living in the Gutenberg House now, so he moved back into his childhood home. Once again, his money had run out, but he was determined to

A page from Donatus, *a school grammar book, which was Johannes Gutenberg's first book printed on his printing press*

continue printing. This time, he borrowed money from his cousin Arnold Gelthus.

With this money, Gutenberg worked to perfect the mechanical functions of his press to make sure it worked as perfectly as possible. Next, he had to decide what to print. It is believed that he experimented first with one or two small printing projects. In about 1450, he printed his first book, a common school grammar book called *Ars Grammatica*. The book is usually referred to as the *Donatus* after its author, Aelius Donatus. To save money, Gutenberg crammed the letters and the words close together on each page. The book was not elaborate, just a lot of thick, fancy Gothic letters without decoration. Gutenberg also printed a poem from what was called the *Sibylline Prophecies*. A small postcard-sized scrap of paper is all that remains of it. The *Donatus* and poem were good sellers in Germany.

Gutenberg had a much bigger project in mind, however—one only a few would have attempted. He planned to print the entire Bible in the Latin language, using movable type and his printing presses. To do this, he would need more money.

Again, he approached someone about a loan. In 1450, he convinced Johannes Fust, a wealthy businessman and lawyer, to loan him 800 guldens, a large amount of money that would have bought several farms at that time. For Fust to agree to such a

Johannes Gutenberg (front) and his partner Johann Fust with the printing press

large sum, Gutenberg must have convinced him that his project, the biggest undertaking of his life, would be profitable. Perhaps he showed Fust his printing press and told him of his plans. Perhaps he convinced him that the Bible would be a big seller, especially in the Roman Catholic Church.

Fust was convinced, and he loaned Gutenberg the money. Gutenberg continued to work on his project, but two years later, in 1452, he was again out of money. Once more, he approached Fust, who agreed to advance him another 800 guldens. In today's money, the two loans would amount to hundreds of thousands of dollars.

However, Fust was a careful and clever businessman. Not only was he a lawyer and a goldsmith, but he was also a professional money lender who made a business out of giving people loans. Of course, he also knew that he should protect himself in case a client failed to pay back a loan.

Fust protected his loan to Gutenberg by asking him to sign an agreement that made them partners. The agreement also stated that Gutenberg had to pay back the loan, plus interest, in at least five years. In addition, if Gutenberg did not repay the loan, Fust would get everything—the presses, the bars of type, the molds, the formulas for the ink, the paper, and printed pages.

Eager to get back to his project, Gutenberg readily signed the document. He was willing to sign anything so he could finish his amazing project—a Bible with two columns and 42 lines of text on each page.

A printer, compositor (seated at right), and proofreaders worked in a printing work-shop.

At the end of 1452, when he was about 54 years old, he began the huge task of printing the Bible. His invention was working, as he had long hoped. The type, the chase, the presses, the ink, and the paper were producing pages for the huge book. He worked hard to produce his masterpiece that has ever since been linked to his name—the Gutenberg Bible. By 1455, it was nearly complete. ❧

Incipit prologus sancti iheronimi presbiteri i parabolas salomonis iungat epistola quos iungit sacerdotium: immo carta non diuidat: quos xpi nectit amor. Commentarios in osee. amos: z zachariá malachiá quoq; poscitis. Scripsisse: si licuisset preualitudine. Minimis solacia sumptuum. notarios nros et librarios sustentans: ut vobis potissimum nrm desudet ingeniu. Et ecce ex latere frequens turba diuersa poscentiu: quasi aut equu sit me vobis esurientibus alijs laborare: aut in ratione dati et accepti cuiqz preter vos obnoxius sim. Itaqz longa egrotatione fractus: ne penitus hoc anno reticerem: z apud vos mutus essem: triduo opus nomini vro consecraui: interpretatione videlicet triu salomonis voluminu: masloth qd hebrei pabolas. vulgata editio puibia vocat: coeleth. quem greci ecclesiasten latine contionatorem possumus dicere: sirasirim: qd i linguá nram vertit canticu canticor. Fertur et panaretos: iesu filij sirach liber: z alius pseudographus qui sapientia salomonis inscribit. Quorz priore hebraicum reperi: no ecclesiasticu ut apud latinos: sed pabolas pnotatu. Cui iuncti erant ecclesiastes et canticu canticorz: ut similitudine salomonis: no solu numero librorum: sed etiam materiarz genere coequaret. Secundus apud hebreos nusqz est: quia et ipse stilus grecam eloquentiá redolet: et nonulli scriptorz veteres hunc esse iudei filonis affirmant. Sicut ergo iudith z thobie z machabeorz libros: legit quidé eos ecclesia: sed inter canonicas scripturas no recipit: sic z hec duo volumina legat ad edificatione plebis: no ad auctoritatem ecclesiasticorz dogmatu cōfirmandam.

Si cui sane septuaginta interpretum magis editio placet: habet eá a nobis olim emendata. Neqz eni noua sic cudimus: ut vetera destruamus. Et tamé cū diligentissime legerit: sciat magis nra scripta intelligi: que no in tertiu vas transfusa coacuerit: sed statim de prelo purissime comendata teste: suu saporem seruauerit. Incipiut parabole salomois

Parabole salomonis filij dauid regis isrl': ad sciendā sapientiam z disciplinā: ad intelligenda verba prudentie et suscipiendā eruditionē doctrine: iusticiá et iudiciū z equitaté: ut detur paruulis astutia: et adolescenti scientia et intellectus. Audiēs sapiés sapientior erit: z intelligēs gubernacla possidebit. Aniaduertet parabolam et interpretationem: verba sapientiū z enigmata eorz. Timor dni principiū sapiētie. Sapientiam atqz doctrinam stulti despiciūt. Audi fili mi disciplinā pris tui et ne dimittas legem mris tue: ut addatur gracia capiti tuo: z torques collo tuo. Fili mi si te lactauerint pctores: ne acquiescas eis. Si dixerint veni nobiscū: insidiemur sanguini: abscondamus tēdiculas cōtra insontem frustra: deglutiamus eū sicud infernus viuentē z integrum: quasi descendentē in lacū: omnē preciosā substantiā reperiemus: implebimus domus nras spolijs: sortem mitte nobiscum: marsupiū sit unum omniū nrm: fili mi ne ambules cū eis. Prohibe pedem tuū a semitis eorz. Pedes eni illorz ad malu currūt: z festināt ut effundant sanguinem. Frustra autem iacitur rete ante oculos pēnatorz. Ipi qz cōtra sanguinē suū insidiantur: et

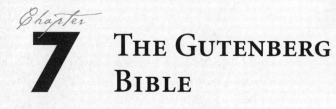

Chapter
7 THE GUTENBERG BIBLE

⦾⁓⦿⁓⦾

Gutenberg's Bible was a marvel of technology and a beautiful work of art. It was truly a masterpiece. The letters were perfectly formed, not fuzzy or smudged. They were all the same height and stood tall and straight on the page. The 42 lines of text were spaced evenly in two perfect columns. The large versals were bright, colorful, and artistic. Some pages had more colorful artwork weaving around the two columns of text.

Gutenberg must have been pleased with his handiwork. But he wouldn't have known then that this Bible would be considered one of the most beautiful books ever printed.

He chose a monumental task for one of his first printed books. Perhaps he wanted to create some-

A page of Gutenberg's Bible with 42 lines of text

thing important that would be remembered after his life was over. Perhaps he wanted to help the Roman Catholic Church by providing an accurate Latin version of the Bible, the most important religious book for the church.

> *Most scribes were monks who worked in a copying room called a scriptorium. Because they believed they should make their books beautiful for the glory of God, the monks formed letters, words, and decorations very carefully. Fearing that a fire would destroy all their hard work, they refused to light candles and labored only during daylight hours. They refused to have a fireplace in the scriptorium, so they worked in the cold. The monks decorated large capital letters and the borders of pages with miniature scenes, vines, flowers, and paintings of people and animals.*

At that time, Catholic priests throughout Europe were using many different versions of the Bible. Since Bibles were copied by hand, each one was unique. Local priests and scribes who copied them sometimes made mistakes. At times, they even changed words and sentences on purpose to make the text fit their own personal religious beliefs.

German Cardinal Nicholas of Cusa, one of the top leaders in the Roman Catholic Church, was concerned about this. For several years, he had been working to unite all Roman Catholics as well as Christians all over the world. Using Bibles that contained different information only led to more disunity and divisions in churches everywhere.

Nicholas believed that every

priest and every church should have an accurate Bible that never changed. He wanted the libraries in all the Roman Catholic monasteries to have a correct copy of the holy text. That way, all priests

Nicholas of Cusa (1401-1464), German cardinal of the Roman Catholic Church

would use the same Bible in their studies and in their churches.

Nicholas visited Mainz in May 1451 to meet with 70 abbots, the priests in charge of the monasteries throughout Europe. He came to talk to them about unity and the importance of having a common edition of the Bible. Perhaps Gutenberg was aware of the cardinal's visit. It is even possible that Nicholas and Gutenberg met and discussed the printing of one accurate version of the Bible.

Somehow, Gutenberg knew it would be acceptable and profitable to print a Bible. It would have to be a version that was satisfactory to the religious leaders of the Catholic Church. Most important, the pope, the head of the Roman Catholic Church, would have to approve it. This would guarantee that Gutenberg's Bible would be acceptable to all Catholic churches, monasteries, and convents. It would also ensure plenty of sales and repeat orders. Printing a book that would be used throughout Europe would make his venture a real success. It would also make him a very important person.

If this is why Gutenberg decided to print the Bible, it explains why he struggled to compose it in Latin, the language used in the Roman Catholic Church. He carefully looked for mistakes and made sure printed copies were correct. Gutenberg had to be well educated in the Latin language in order to produce a Bible in perfect Latin.

To complete his huge task, Gutenberg hired Peter Schöffer, an expert scribe, as his assistant. Gutenberg told him to make the text look like the handwritten Gothic letters used by scribes. Schöffer drew a beautiful sample of each letter of the alphabet. Under Gutenberg's instruction, he learned how

Scribes copied books using a quill pen and parchment; scribes were fine artists who also drew beautiful designs throughout the text.

to make the punches, the handheld molds, and the finished type look just like his design. The final printed pages were masterfully done. When the first pages came out, some people did not believe they were made by a machine. They looked like hand-written manuscripts.

Printing the Bible was a massive and expensive operation. Gutenberg had to pay workers to mold the type, place the type in a chase, and run the printing presses. More large presses had to be made,

A replica of Gutenberg's printing press is on display at the Gutenberg Museum in Mainz, Germany.

more metal had to be delivered, and enough paper and parchment had to be purchased. Gutenberg was extremely precise about how the finished pages should look. He insisted that some work be thrown away and printed again, even if it cost extra money to do it.

It took several years for Gutenberg's 20 workers to print about 175 copies of his 1,282-page Bible. It probably took the first two years just to prepare the type and the chases for printing. A chase for each page contained more than 2,000 letters, with about 290 different types of letters, symbols, and spaces on one page. Gutenberg's team ran six presses at a time and printed the same page on all the presses until all of the 175 copies of that page were finished.

Of the 175 copies, 135 were printed on paper and 40 on parchment. The parchment Bibles were special copies that would sell for a lot of money to the wealthy and the churches. More than 5,000 animal skins were used to produce these 40 special editions. The paper copies required about 50,000 sheets of paper that measured 16 by 12 inches (40.6 by 30 centimeters). Once the pages were printed, colorful initials, designs, and borders were added by an artist called an illuminator. The pages of the Bible would then have to be sewn together in the middle with strong thread and bound into two large volumes with covers.

Johannes Gutenberg looks at the first page to be printed using his printing press; it is being lifted from metal type in a chase.

Printing these mammoth volumes was an immense undertaking. With his vision, organization, artistic skill, and creativity, Gutenberg held it all together. His workshop was undoubtedly a very busy place while the Bible was being printed.

Imagine six compositors [people who place type for text] and twelve printers, two to a press, positioning the typeset metal pages, laying on the ink with their fat, soft, powder-puff-shaped leather ink-balls, positioning the paper or vellum, sliding the carriage into position, winding down the press, feeling for just the right amount of pressure.

Gutenberg's men worked on all stages of the process, day in and day out. The finished pages were amazing, truly a marriage of technology and art. ✍

8 FINAL YEARS

હ્ર૰ર

Gutenberg was probably too busy to imagine what was about to happen to him in the middle of 1455. As the 57-year-old printer worked feverishly in Mainz to finish the Bible, the unthinkable happened. At the brink of fame and fortune, just when he was about to present his masterpiece to the Roman Catholic Church and to the world, it all ended.

Fust, the man who had twice loaned Gutenberg huge sums of money for his invention, decided to demand the loan be repaid immediately. There was no way Gutenberg could do that, so Fust sued him for his money. Gutenberg had no resources and no way to fight Fust and win. All the money was tied up in the products, equipment, and partially finished Bible. The agreement, signed by Fust and Gutenberg years before, stated clearly that if the debt could not be repaid, the equipment and materials would belong to Fust.

Hearings were held, and witnesses testified. At first, Gutenberg attended the hearings to plead his case. He emphasized that this was a joint venture for mutual benefit and hoped he wouldn't have to pay the debt yet. After a few hearings, a final hearing was scheduled. Fust would be awarded everything if Gutenberg didn't come forth to successfully challenge the claim.

The final hearing was scheduled for Thursday, November 6, 1455, at the Convent of the Barefoot Friars, near the cathedral in Mainz. The hearing took place with a small group of people. Helmasperger, the notary, wrote down what was being said, while a few witnesses stood nearby. Gutenberg's assistant, Peter Schöffer, was there with Fust and Jakob, Fust's brother. There was a hush in the room as the people in the courtroom waited for Gutenberg to arrive. Fust was getting impatient.

There was no sign of Gutenberg. Three men entered the room—the former minister of St. Christopher's Church, Gutenberg's house servant Heinrich Keffer, and Heinrich's son Bechtolf von Hanau. Gutenberg still was not there. Fust insisted that the proceedings begin. The claim was read along with Gutenberg's arguments, and the hearing

A notary writes down what the judge says in a 15th-century court.

went on without Gutenberg there to defend himself. Gutenberg must have sensed that the final outcome would be in Fust's favor. Perhaps he wanted to stay back in his workshop in order to face defeat privately if he lost.

Finally, the verdict was read. Gutenberg would have to repay the debt or give everything to Fust. Now the technology and the art would be handed over to a man who had not had any part in creating them. Everything—the stacks of beautifully printed pages, the presses, the chases, the metal bars of type, the ink— belonged to Fust.

Was it unfair of Fust to demand the debt be paid in the final hour of Gutenberg's project? Did he do this to take it all away from Gutenberg, steal the credit, and make his own fortune? Had he planned this ahead of time? Or did he finally give up on Gutenberg ever making enough to repay his money and simply ask for his debt to be repaid? Whatever his reason, Fust would not be remembered favorably for what he did.

Since Gutenberg had no way to pay his debt, Fust gathered up

Gutenberg's invention sparked the opposite of what he probably intended. Hoping to help the Roman Catholic Church stay united, he printed the Bible, believing that churches throughout Europe would use the same holy text. Instead, the Bible was translated into many languages. This meant that people could read the Bible in their own language and study it without the guidance of priests. People who studied the Bible on their own began to criticize the Roman Catholic Church. This eventually led to the Protestant Reformation.

all of Gutenberg's equipment and the thousands of printed pages. Schöffer and others who had worked for Gutenberg joined Fust in a new printing business. Together, they finished putting together the Bible and printing more copies. They did what Gutenberg had intended to do—print a Bible that would provide one version of the holy scriptures to the Roman Catholic Church and unite the priests.

Fust and Schöffer gained fame for the books they printed on Gutenberg's presses. Unlike Gutenberg, Fust and Schöffer included a printer's mark called a colophon, a type of unique logo, on books they made. The first book to include their

A Gutenberg Bible, opened to the book of Ecclesiastes

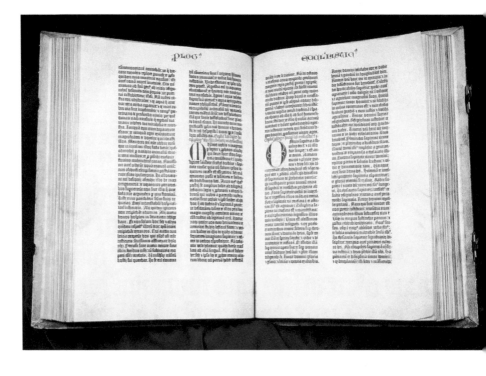

printer's mark was a copy of a Latin *Psalter*, or Psalms from the Bible. They not only indicated they had printed the book, but they also took credit for inventing the printing method. No credit was given to Gutenberg. Their statement read:

> *The present copy of the Psalms ... was so fashioned thanks to the ingenious discovery of imprinting and forming letters without any use of a pen and completed with diligence to the glory of God by Johann Fust, citizen of Mainz, and Peter Schöffer of Gernsheim.*

Part of the first page of the Latin Psalter, *printed by German printers Schöffer and Fust*

It wasn't long before many of the men who had

worked for Gutenberg started their own printing businesses. Printing workshops filled with printing presses sprang up all over Europe. These presses duplicated Gutenberg's invention but at no profit to him, since patents to protect someone's invention did not exist.

Fust and Schöffer went on to become a successful team. Even after Fust died of the plague in 1466, Schöffer continued the business for nearly 40 years. He died rich and respected in 1503.

When Gutenberg lost his printing press, he was faced with the decision to either give up his life's dream or start over. He managed to start again, this time on a much smaller scale. The difficult part had already been done. The research, development, and techniques had been worked out, and very few people knew all the details of his art and craft. Gutenberg was an amazing person who was not willing to quit.

> *He may have been knocked into a daze by this catastrophic blow to his ego. He may have been almost sixty years old. But whatever he was, he was Gutenberg, a man who had started many things at many different times of his life. He was not ready to give up.*

Within two years, Gutenberg built a new workshop, designed and molded new type, and printed another edition of the Bible, this time with 36 lines to a page. With fewer lines, this Bible was easier to read but had more pages. As usual, Gutenberg did not indicate who the printer was.

Gutenberg also printed more copies of the *Donatus* and an astronomical calendar showing the phases of the moon on certain dates. Around 1460, he printed the *Catholicon*, a large Latin dictionary and encyclopedia.

At the end of this book are Gutenberg's own words:

The type from Gutenberg's 36-line Bible was larger than his first Bible that had 42 lines on each page.

[T]his noble book Catholicon ... *without the help of reed, stylus or pen, but by the wondrous agreement, proportion and harmony of punches and types has been printed and brought to an end.*

These may be the only words we actually know that Gutenberg wrote.

In 1462, the political climate in Mainz was again not good. After a fierce battle among the citizens, Adolf, the Roman Catholic archbishop in Mainz, ordered people to leave. Among them was Gutenberg, who escaped with some of his equipment to Eltville, the same place he and his family had fled when he was a boy. Gutenberg's niece lived there, as did some of his friends.

In 1465, when Gutenberg was about 69, Adolf invited him to return to Mainz. He encouraged Gutenberg to continue his printing operations. Printing had become very important in Europe. It was to Adolf's benefit to be associated with a man who knew so much about printing. Gutenberg received an income from Adolf until his death, but he was never able to pay off all of his debts.

When Gutenberg returned to Mainz in 1465, he knew his

In Mainz, in 1461, there arose a conflict over two archbishops of the Roman Catholic Church. Most of the people wanted Diether von Isenburg to lead them, but Adolf II had been appointed leader of Mainz by the pope, the head of the Catholic Church. In 1462, Adolf II attacked the city of Mainz, killing 400 citizens. He took all the property from those who survived and divided it among those who promised to follow him. Those who would not follow him (among them Johannes Gutenberg) were forced to leave the city or be put in prison.

Present-day Germany
Map shows boundaries
of the 1400s.

North Sea

DENMARK

ENGLAND

Berlin

Elbe River

Rhine River

FLANDERS

HOLY ROMAN EMPIRE

Eltville
Mainz

Main River

N
W · E
S

English
Lands

Paris

Seine River

Strasbourg

Rhine R.

Ill River

Danube River

Munich

Lake
Constance

BURGUNDY

SWITZERLAND

Lake
Geneva

FRANCE

| 0 | | 90 miles |
| 0 | | 90 kilometers |

Gutenberg lived in Mainz, Germany, and Strasbourg (now in France)

invention had taken the city by storm. Printing shops there were producing books as fast as possible. Citizens were buying books and reading more. Gutenberg didn't know that he would be remembered in history for this printing industry that was the rage of the Renaissance and was changing the world. But for the next three years, he would at least see how his printing process changed his city.

On February 3, 1468, Gutenberg died and was buried at the Convent of the Barefoot Friars in Mainz, Germany, in an unmarked grave. He was laid to rest at the place where everything had been taken from him 13 years before. ✑

9 Chapter IMPRINT ON HISTORY

❧❦❧

Almost 600 years after Gutenberg's death, the Gutenberg Bible stands out as one of the most astounding objects ever created. Today, 48 copies of his 42-line Bible remain. Two are owned by the Gutenberg Museum in Mainz and the other 46 are spread throughout the world in Belgium, Denmark, Germany, France, Great Britain, Vatican City, Japan, Austria, Poland, Portugal, Russia, Switzerland, Spain, and the United States.

Twenty-seven of those remaining copies are ones that were printed on parchment. Three of the parchment volumes are in the Library of Congress in Washington, D.C.; two are in New York City at the Pierpont Morgan Library; and two are in the Huntington Library in San Marino, California.

Statue of Johannes Gutenberg in Strasbourg, in present-day France

These beautiful masterpieces of Gutenberg's creation attract many visitors every year. They want to see the amazing quality of one of the first books to be printed using movable type.

> *It still appears miraculous that this first typographic book in Europe ... should be of such sublime beauty and mastery that later generations up to our own day have rarely matched and never excelled it in quality.*

Gutenberg was the right man in the right place at the right time. Fifteenth-century Europe was hungry for knowledge and new ideas. Interest in the arts, languages, literature, and history had increased. Paper was being made in Europe. Scientists were beginning to question old ideas and make exciting new discoveries. With the invention of the printing press, Gutenberg set off an explosion—an explosion of books—that was felt around the Western world.

In the 45 years after Gutenberg perfected his printing press and printed the Bible, from 1455 to 1500, more than 10 million books were printed. By the year 1501, there were 1,120 print shops in 260 towns in 17 European countries. Because of the power of the printed word, a new era of learning and knowledge was at its peak. The invention of printing helped fuel the Renaissance, the era of great learn-

A French printing shop in the 1500s

ing in literature, science, and the arts.

Before the printing press, people learned from a limited number of sources. They didn't have their own books, so they were taught by those who owned handwritten books. Once printing made books available, people thirsted for knowledge like never before in history. Printed books gave people the chance to learn, explore new ideas, and share knowledge quickly. Through books, they learned practical skills, gained information about the world, and became aware of scientific discoveries.

Gutenberg has received acclaim and praise for what he did for people throughout the world. One historian wrote:

Gutenberg's printing press affected all of Europe and eventually the whole world by giving people access to books and more knowledge.

Johann Gutenberg provided mankind with what may well be the most significant single tool ever invented—the tool whereby the thoughts, hopes, anxieties, and ideas of men may be communicated through all time.

Much has been written about the impact of the printing press on the world. Printing was both an invention and an event. It gave birth to a period of time when people could educate themselves and learn more about the world.

What we read today—newspapers, magazines, books, signs, and posters—is the result of the invention of printing. Even maps, postage stamps, and the labels on products we buy are possible because of what Gutenberg did. The arrival of printing in the mid-15th century set off a revolution that was felt in all major areas of life: education, politics, religion, and language.

Not long after Gutenberg's death, people started giving him credit for the invention of the printing press. On December 31, 1470, the rector of the University of Paris praised the inventor in a letter:

> *Not far from the city of Mainz, there appeared a certain Johann whose surname was Gutenberg, who, first of all men, devised the art of printing, whereby books are made, not by a reed, as did the ancients, nor with a quill pen, as do we, but with metal letters, and that swiftly, neatly, beautifully. Surely this man is worthy to be loaded with divine honors by all the Muses, all the arts, all the tongues of those who delight in books.*

Gutenberg holds his Bible in one hand and a bar of movable type in the other.

Thirty-five years later, in 1505, Schöffer's son made a public statement that gave Gutenberg full credit for the invention of printing. He acknowledged Gutenberg's work in a public speech in which he referred to a book that was printed at Mainz. Part of the speech referred to "the town in which the admirable art of typography was invented, in the year 1450, by Johann Gutenberg."

Although Gutenberg changed the world, he was buried in an unmarked grave. No one placed a headstone or an engraved memorial where he was put to rest. But a distant cousin, Adam Gelthus, later wrote a memorial to this man who put his imprint on history:

> *To Johann Gensfleisch*
> *Inventor of the art of printing*
> *Deserver of the best from all nations*
> *and tongues*
> *To the immortal memory of his name*
> *Adam Gelthus places [this memorial].*
> *His remains rest peacefully*
> *In the church of St. Francis, Mainz.*

Gutenberg left an even bigger memorial: "the greatest memorial of all, the work of the books, which was already starting to change the world." His name became forever linked with his masterpiece—the Gutenberg Bible—and with the printing press, the invention that transformed the world. ❧

GUTENBERG'S LIFE

1410

Flees with his
family to Eltville,
the family's
country estate

1419

His father dies

1398

Born in Mainz,
Germany

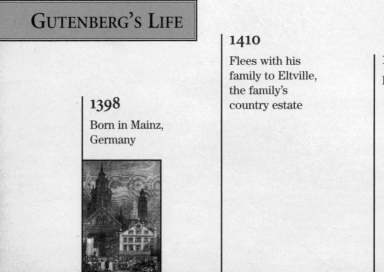

1395

1415

1399

Henry IV
becomes king
of England

1415

John Hus is burned
at the stake for
speaking out
against the Roman
Catholic Church

WORLD EVENTS

1428

Leaves Mainz for
Strasbourg after
guilds take over the
city council

1434

Visits Mainz
to attend his
mother's
funeral

1437

Teaches stone
polishing to
Andreas Dritzehn

1430

1431

Eugenius IV becomes
pope of the Roman
Catholic Church

GUTENBERG'S LIFE

1448

Establishes
printing shop
in Mainz

1450

Prints the *Donatus*;
borrows money from
Johann Fust

1438

Forms partnership
with three others to
produce mirrors for
pilgrimage

1450

1441

Jan van Eyck,
Dutch painter, dies

1450

Vatican Library
is founded

WORLD EVENTS

1452-1455

Prints the 42-line Bible in two volumes

1452

Forms partnership with Johann Fust

1455

Loses court case and all his work and equipment to Fust

1455

1452

Leonardo da Vinci is born

1455–1487

War of the Roses is fought in England

GUTENBERG'S LIFE

1462

Flees to Eltville

1458-1460

Prints the 36-line
Bible

ñuîtatis ïueſtigabo: et ponâ ï
lumen ſcïentiã illius·ꝛ non pte=
ribo.veritate : neꝗ cum ïuidia

1460

1460

Winchester Cathedral
in England is
completed

WORLD EVENTS

1468

Dies in Mainz, Germany, on February 3

1465

Returns to Mainz with a pension to live on

1465

1465

The first piece of music is printed

1466

Johann Mentel prints the first German Bible

DATE OF BIRTH: c. 1398

ALSO KNOWN AS: Johann Gensfleisch,
Johann Gensfleischzur,
Laden zum Gutenberg

BIRTHPLACE: Mainz, Germany

FATHER: Friele Gensfleisch zur
Laden (c. 1350–1419)

MOTHER: Else Wirich Gutenberg
(?–1433)

EDUCATION: Unknown

DATE OF DEATH: February 3, 1468

PLACE OF BURIAL: Convent of the Barefoot
Friars, Mainz, Germany

In the Library

Burch, Joann Johansen. *Fine Print: A Story About Johann Gutenberg*. Minneapolis: Carolrhoda Books, 1991.

Fisher, Leonard Everett. *Gutenberg*. New York: Macmillan, 1993.

Langley, Andrew. *Eyewitness: Medieval Life*. New York: Alfred A. Knopf, 1996.

Steffens, Bradley. *Printing Press: Ideas Into Type (Encyclopedia of Discovery and Invention)*. San Diego, Calif.: Lucent Books, 1990.

Thorpe, James. *The Gutenberg Bible: Landmark in Learning*. San Marino, Calif.: Huntington Library Press, 1999.

Look for more Signature Lives books about this era:

Christopher Columbus: *Explorer of the New World*

Nicolaus Copernicus: *Father of Modern Astronomy*

Elizabeth I: *Queen of Tudor England*

Galileo: *Astronomer and Physicist*

Michelangelo: *Sculptor and Painter*

Francisco Pizarro: *Conqueror of the Incas*

William Shakespeare: *Playwright and Poet*

ON THE WEB

For more information on *Johannes Gutenberg*, use FactHound to track down Web sites related to this book.

1. Go to *www.facthound.com*
2. Type in a search word related to this book or this book ID: 0756509890
3. Click on the *Fetch It* button.

FactHound will find the best Web sites for you.

HISTORIC SITES

Great Hall of the Library of Congress
Jefferson Building
10 First St., S.E.
Washington, DC 20540-1610
202/707-2905
To view one of the original copies of the Gutenberg Bible

Gutenberg Museum
Liebfrauenplatz 5
Mainz, Germany 55116
011 49 (06131) 12 26 40
To view a re-creation of Gutenberg's printing press

abbots
the monks in charge of monasteries

bubonic plague
a fatal disease with painful swelling of the lymph glands and a darkening of the skin

cardinal
an official of the Roman Catholic Church next in rank to the pope

chase
a frame used to hold metal type in place

convent
a building where a group of religious women live

exiled
sent away or cast out

guild
a group of merchants or craftsmen, especially before 1500, that worked in the same trade

guldens
plural for guilder, a coin formerly used as money in Germany, Austria, and the Netherlands

illuminated manuscripts
pages of books decorated with gold or silver and brilliant colors

matrix
the metal mold for type made with hot metal

metallurgy
the study of metals

mint
a place where coins are made

monasteries
buildings where men live and study to devote themselves to their religious vows

monks
men who live in a monastery to devote themselves
to their religious vows

parchment
in former times, a material made from dried and
treated animal hide, used to write on

pilgrimage
a journey to a holy place, for religious reasons

press
a machine used to push inked metal type against a
sheet of paper

punch
a tool with a raised letter carved at one end

rector
a member of the Roman Catholic clergy in charge
of a congregation, college, or religious community

relief
the elevation of shapes from a flat surface

scribes
people who copy manuscripts by hand

scriptorium
a room in a monastery for copying, illustrating,
reading, and storing manuscripts

spacers
blank metal bars of various widths used to make
spaces in printed text

vellum
fine parchment made from the skin of a newly
born calf, sheep, or goat

versal
a large, colorful letter at the beginning of a
chapter in a book

Chapter 4

Page 42, line 9: John Man. *Gutenberg: How One Man Remade the World With Words*. New York: John Wiley, 2002, p. 56.

Page 46, line 6: Joann Johansen Burch. *Fine Print: A Story About Johann Gutenberg*. Minneapolis: Carolrhoda Books, 1991, p. 40.

Chapter 7

Page 75, line 1: *Gutenberg: How One Man Remade the World With Words*, pp. 175-176.

Chapter 8

Page 82, line 6: Ibid., p. 194.

Page 83, line 19: Brayton Harris. *Johann Gutenberg and the Invention of Printing*. New York: Franklin Watts, 1972, p. 115.

Chapter 9

Page 90, line 5: Albert Kapr. *Johann Gutenberg: The Man and His Invention*. Translated from the German by Douglas Martin. Brookfield, Vt.: Scholar Press, 1996, p. 165.

Page 92, line 4: *Johann Gutenberg and the Invention of Printing*, p. 133.

Page 93, line 18: James Thorpe. *The Gutenberg Bible: Landmark in Learning*. San Marino, Calif.: Huntington Library Press, 1999, pp. 30-31.

Page 95, line 3: Leonard Everett Fisher. *Gutenberg*. New York: Macmillan, 1993, (pages unnumbered).

Page 95, line 12: *Gutenberg: How One Man Remade the World With Words*, p. 214.

Page 95, line 20: Ibid.

Burke, James, and Robert E. Ornstein. *The Axemaker's Gift: Technology's Capture and Control of Our Minds and Culture*. New York: Tarcher/Putnam, 1997.

Burns, Edward McNall, Robert E. Lerner, and Standish Meacham. *Western Civilizations: Their History and Their Culture*. New York: W.W. Norton, 1980.

De Hamel, Christopher. *A History of Illuminated Manuscripts*. London: Phaidon Press Limited, 1994.

Eisenstein, Elizabeth L. *The Printing Revolution in Early Modern Europe*. Cambridge, Mass.: Cambridge University Press, 1983.

Fisher, Leonard Everett. *Gutenberg*. New York: Macmillan, 1993.

Fromkin, David. *The Way of the World: From the Dawn of Civilizations to the Eve of the Twenty-First Century*. New York: Alfred A. Knopf, 1999.

Johns, Adrian. *The Nature of the Book: Print and Knowledge in the Making*. Chicago, Ill.: University of Chicago Press, 1998.

Kapr, Albert. *Johann Gutenberg: The Man and His Invention*. Translated from the German by Douglas Martin. Brookfield, Vt.: Scholar Press, 1996.

Krensky, Stephen. *Breaking Into Print: Before and After the Invention of the Printing Press*. Boston: Little, Brown and Company, 1996.

Man, John. Gutenberg: *How One Man Remade the World With Words*. New York: John Wiley, 2002.

McMurtrie, Douglas C., and Don Farran. *Wings for Words: The Story of Johann Gutenberg and His Invention of Printing*. New York: Rand McNally, 1940.

Thorpe, James. *The Gutenberg Bible: Landmark in Learning*. San Marino, Calif.: Huntington Library Press, 1999.

Fran Rees is the author of many books and has taught music and English at the elementary and junior high school levels. She keeps extensive written and art journals of her life and interests. She lives in Mesa, Arizona, with her husband and daughter.

Image Credits